Fashion Style Book

Written and edited by Robyn Newton, Gillian Henney, and Amy Marks

Illustrations courtesy of the Bonnie Marcus Collection

Designed by Claire Brisley

Fashion Consultant: Meg Rysk DeCubellis, Senior Critic of Apparel Design at RISD

Production by Jack Aylward

This edition published by Parragon Books Ltd in 2014 and distributed by

Parragon Inc.
440 Park Avenue South, 13th Floor
New York, NY 10016
www.parragon.com

ISBN 978-1-4723-3883-9

Printed in China

Fashion Style Book

PaRragon

Bath · New York · Cologne · Melbourne · Delhi
Hong Kong · Shenzhen · Singapore · Amsterdam

Contents

Design It

About Bonnie Marcus

Bonnie Marcus launched her stylish stationery company, the Bonnie Marcus Collection "where fashion meets paper®," in 2002 from her dining room table, while expecting her first child. As a former wedding planner in New York City, Marcus was well-known for her event planning expertise and found there was a void in the stationery market in terms of fashion-forward stylish designs. She decided to combine her passion for fashion (having worked for designer Diane Von Furstenberg) with her love of event planning and her collection took the stationery industry by storm! Bonnie's stylish designs are now available in thousands of retail stores worldwide and celebrity fans include Cindy Crawford, Christina Aguilera, Britney Spears, Eva Longoria, Marcia Cross, and many others. Marcus has been recognized as a pioneer for women in business and is proud to be an established partner of the Breast Cancer Research Foundation® and Autism Speaks®. For further information about the company, please visit www.bonniemarcus.com.

Your Fashion Style Book

This is about making YOUR own fashion choices. Step inside the rocking universe of fashion … Design, scrapbook, snap selfies, and scribble down your stylish moments of inspiration.

FORGET THOSE FASHION FAILS, CREATE YOUR OWN DRESS CODE AND MAKE FASHION WORK YOUR WAY.

The world is

WHAT YOU'LL GET:

THE ULTIMATE CLOSET INSPIRATION TO

transform your style to A-list!

TIPS AND TRICKS TO KEEP YOU

one step ahead of the style set.

TIMELESS FASHION KNOW-HOW TO

whip your closet into shape.

DECADES OF BEST-DRESSED ERAS TO

fast-track your fashion credentials.

TOP DESIGNERS TO PUT AT THE TOP OF YOUR

fashion homework list!

your runway ...

Chanel

Even if you don't think you know any of Gabrielle 'Coco' Chanel's creations, you do! Chanel completely changed women's fashion with her chic suits and LBDs (aka the 'little black dress'). Her designs have inspired just about everyone!

See pages 30–31 for tips on how to wear the LBD.

Sew Coco

Gabrielle Chanel was raised in an orphanage, but it was here that she learned how to sew. After a brief career as a singer, where she got the cute nickname 'Coco,' she opened her first boutique at 31 Rue Cambon, Paris.

Rule Breaker

Chanel was a style rebel, breaking boundaries and traditions to champion her designs. From a love of black to a hatred of tight corsets, Chanel changed the fashion world for the better. We can totally thank her for believing that 'luxury must be comfortable, otherwise it is not luxury.'

Chanel even made it easy for us to follow her rule-breaker style today. Wearing one of her bouclé suit jackets with jeans and a white T-shirt will totally get you noticed for effortless chic.

Iconic Style

We can't overlook the iconic No. 5 perfume as well as the classic 2.55 bag either. They are fashion staples! And the Chanel brand is still creating upscale fashion today. Chief designer Karl Lagerfeld took over in 1983 and continues to keep this super-elegant fashion label true to its founder.

Her life

1883:	Gabrielle "Coco" Bonheur Chanel born in France
1919:	Opens her first store
1921:	Launches the fragrance Chanel No. 5
1926:	Makes the Little Black Dress a classic
1955:	Launches her famous 2.55 quilted handbag
1971:	Dies at the age of 87
1983:	Karl Lagerfeld becomes Chanel's designer

Chanel No.5 perfume

"A girl should be two things: Classy and fabulous."

Coco Chanel

Prada

If you gave your fave brands playground status, Prada would be the cool kid. It may be a century old, but it's still totally trendsetting today! Set up by Italian Mario Prada and his brother Martino as a leather goods store, the label is now a superluxe fashion brand with bags of class!

The Saffiano tote bag

We Run the World!

Mario believed that women and business did not mix, but his daughter Luisa Prada soon changed that! She stepped up to run the family business, making the brand a female powerhouse, and her daughter has now taken over. Prada is crazy successful and has been run by women for over 50 years!

Stylishly Subtle

Forget bold, shouty logos—Prada prefers the understated, classy approach. However, it does have its signature styles, including the famous black Saffiano bag that landed in the 1980s and is still being made today.

Movie Star

Prada was catapulted to OMG must-have status when the novel *The Devil Wears Prada* was published by Lauren Weisberger in 2003, and again when the movie starring Anne Hathaway rocked the box office.

The brand

1913: Prada is founded by Mario Prada

1958: Luisa Prada takes over from her father Mario

1978: Miuccia Prada takes on the brand

1989: Prada womenswear line starts

1993: Miuccia creates a second, less expensive line called Miu Miu (her nickname!)

" *I love clothes. Maybe I can say I don't love fashion, but I love clothes completely.*"

Miuccia Prada

Gucci

Hello Gucci! Meet the brand of popular culture—just flash that double G logo and you'll get immediate street cred. This is one fresh and contemporary, hundred-year-old Italian brand!

The iconic Bamboo Bag

Make Mine Two Gs

Someone named Guccio Gucci is destined for great things, right? In 1921, Guccio started a handbag and suitcase business in Florence. His son Aldo designed a logo, showcasing two interlocking Gs—his dad's initials. Today, THAT logo and the iconic horsebit are instantly recognizable.

Fashionable Family

Guccio's sons took over the label in the late 1940s and soon everyone who was anyone had a Gucci bag, from actress Elizabeth Taylor to Queen Elizabeth II. Aldo's son Paolo took the business to superbrand status in the late 1960s when he introduced women's clothing.

Classic Gucci horsebit loafer

New Generation

Fashion designer and film director Tom Ford started designing for Gucci in 1990. He built on the brand's reputation with jaw-dropping collections and by 1999 had turned Gucci into a $4.3 billion empire!

The brand

1921: Gucci is founded in Florence, Italy

1974: Gucci launches No. 1, the brand's first perfume

1994: Tom Ford is named Creative Director

2004: Tom Ford leaves the Gucci Group

2005: Frida Giannini takes over as creative director of women's ready-to-wear

2011: Gucci opens its own museum in Florence

" *We are living in a material world, so why not live with something beautiful?* "

Tom Ford

Dior

If you had to pick a brand that revolutionized women's wear, it would be Christian Dior! When the couturier presented his first fashion show on February 12, 1947, he didn't realize he was creating a powerhouse brand that would rule the fashion world for decades.

Quintessential modern Dior footwear

Hat Trick

Before following his design dream, Dior worked in an art gallery as an illustrator and served as a military officer in World War II. He began his fashion career selling sketches of hats to Parisians in 1935.

The New Look

Dior unveiled his "New Look" collection right after the war. Women had been trapped in dull, practical clothes for years, so a collection that boasted nipped-in waists, HUGE skirts, and super-feminine shapes totally wowed the crowds. The head-to-toe collection included hats, furs, jewelry, gloves, stockings, shoes, lipstick, and perfume.

Over to Yves

Dior died in 1957 so it was left to his 21-year-old assistant, Yves Saint Laurent, to design the new collection. The clothes were still totally Dior in style, but so much more wearable. Women everywhere rejoiced! J'adore Dior!

The brand

1946: Christian Dior is founded

1947: Dior's "New Look" changes fashion forever!

1956: Dior's tenth anniversary

1957: Yves Saint Laurent takes over, followed by other designers

1996: John Galliano becomes head designer

2011: John Galliano is replaced with Raf Simons

" The real proof of an elegant woman is what is on her feet."

Christian Dior

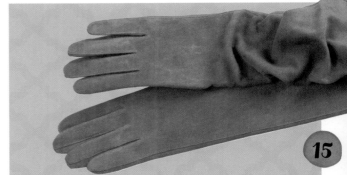

15

Rewind Fashion 1920s

In the 'Roaring Twenties' fashion got rebellious! Women broke free from the prim and proper outfits they had been used to wearing in favor of looser, more boyish styles. The most fashionable girls were nicknamed 'flappers.'

Think chic and cheeky! From blouses with Peter Pan collars and little cloche hats, the look was understated glam for the daytime. At night, a dropped-waist dress, cute, boyish hairdo, and dark red lipstick meant the 1920s' girl was ready to party!

A classic cloche!

Cute Peter Pan collar

Dancing shoes!

Pearl and crystal necklace

Get the ... flapper look!

Turn heads, vintage-style, with Twenties' headgear! A feather headband will totally top off your look.

Pearl beads were THE accessory of the day. Get yourself some fake pearl beads for Twenties-inspired style, and layer them up—the more the merrier!

Step out in style from another era in a dress with a lower waistline than your natural waist, and even if you aren't dancing the Charleston, you will impress with your flapper style know-how!

Allover sparkle might not be right for a shopping trip, but pick a dreamy dress with sequins or beading detail for your next party and you'll shine like a starlet!

Pick kitten heels with T-bars to add the finishing touch to your flapper outfit—perfect for dancing the night away!

Rewind Fashion

1950s

In the 1950s, companies started producing stuff just for teens … Teen movies, books, music, and clothes! Christian Dior had already set the world in a fashion frenzy with his 'New Look' clothing collection so his full skirts became the staples for 1950s' teen style.

Poodle skirts had adorable dog emblems and were worn with bobby sox (short white socks). Sophisticated saddle shoes were on every girl's wish list, and a pretty ponytail became THE fashionable hairstyle. The 1950s' girl was as cute-as-a-button!

Stylish full skirt

Stylish swimwear

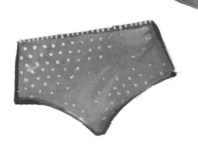

Saddle shoe

Go fabulously... fifties!

A chic silk headscarf was also worn as a hair accessory. Channel your inner 1950s and tie it in a bow for a quick and easy glamor upgrade!

Full skirts were a wardrobe essential! Hunt down a dress with a supersized skirt, or add a netting tutu underneath for an instant 1950s' silhouette.

"Poodle" skirts were supercute with little dog decorations! Take inspiration and look out for skirts or cardigans with cute animal patterns.

Smart flats and short white anklets finished an outfit. Wear them today for an edgy, preppy look.

1960s

The 1960s gave the fashion world an extreme makeover! Hemlines came up, space-age silhouettes came in, and the stores were filled with crazy, head-turning trends.

Supermodel Twiggy was the poster girl for superlong eyelashes, dolly makeup, and short, pixie-cut hair. PVC dresses and go-go boots were in every teen wardrobe, and Mod (modernist) style took over. But the biggest hit was the famous, eye-popping creation by Mary Quant. All bow down to … the miniskirt!

Twiggy

Newsboy hat

Psychedelic mini

Square-toed shoe

Style it the ... Sixties way!

Statement false eyelashes and oversized sunglasses are totally Twiggy!

Black and white is so monochrome Mod! Give your look some geometric style with a color-block dress.

More was definitely more in the 1960s. When picking patterns and colors, don't try to be too matchy-matchy— embrace the clash!

A minidress with long boots is the ultimate in sassy Sixties chic. It will boost your homage to the decade.

1980s

Love a color pop? You'd have been right at home in the 1980s! Forget natural beauty—statement pink lipsticks and blue eyeshadows filled makeup bags everywhere, and accessories were supersized!

Madonna was THE teen fashion icon. Think short skirts, bleached hair, fishnet gloves, hairbows, and long strings of beads. Popular movies of the time, like *Fame*, turned dancewear into everyday wear. And hair was BIG! Seems totally crazy we know, but if it wasn't permed, crimped, or curled to the max, it wasn't on trend!

Madonna in 1984

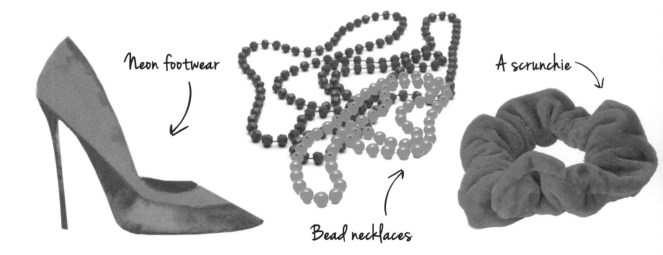

Neon footwear

Bead necklaces

A scrunchie

Step it up ... to the 1980s!

It doesn't come more Eighties than the hair scrunchie. Make it velvet or neon—it's gotta have standout appeal!

Plastic beads screamed fashion in the 1980s. Wear as many as you dare, you know you want to!

Skirts were short, simple as that! Try a raa-raa skirt for big and beautiful impact!

Got some megabright neon leg warmers? Go full-on neon to work dance-studio chic.

High-tops totally completed the look! Go 1980s' streetglam and wear yours with a minidress.

Rewind Fashion 1990s

The 1990s get a bad fashion rep. But don't throw away "the decade fashion forgot" into the trash pile just yet. The Nineties had some style gems that should be filed under "crazy-cool."

In the 1990s, the overstyled try-hard look was out—dressing down was the mantra of the decade. Inspired by bands like Nirvana, grunge was about attitude. Flannel plaid shirts, band T-shirts, and baggy, ripped jeans were in. Even floral babydoll dresses were given cool points with chunky Doc Martens boots.

90s' supermodel Kate Moss

Plaid fabric

Babydoll dress

Doc Martens

Grunge it up ... Nineties style!

Plaid was the overshirt essential. Forget farmer, think 1990s' uberstyle!

A band T-shirt was THE coolest choice—the more battered, the better! Worn with an unbuttoned checked shirt, it became the ultimate in grunge chic.

Distressed jeans and a beanie hat showcased the inner rebel. Mess up your hair and add tons of eyeliner for total grunge impact.

Footwear was all about chunky high-tops and boots. Beef up your footwear for Nineties street cred.

The Leather Jacket

It's a piece that can transform any outfit from 'what was she wearing?' to 'HOW does she do it?' The leather jacket is power dressing at its very best. Invest in quality and you'll look totally on-trend, season after season.

Classic

Tailored shape

Styling Tips

✶ Style up your leather jacket with a cute dress and beaten-up boots for the ultimate in punk meets pretty.

✶ Rock chick at heart? Team your jacket with skinny jeans and a studded belt.

✶ For the funky worn-in look, try thrift stores for some secondhand cool.

Functional Fashion

Leather jackets may scream "biker," but they were actually first made for pilots in World War I. Marlon Brando gave leather a bad boy vibe in the 1953 movie, *The Wild One*, and it quickly became a staple for cool kids worldwide!

Leather goes Designer

Yves Saint Laurent was the first big designer to show a leather jacket on the runway back in 1960 in his "Beat" collection. Today you're certain to find a luxe leather or stylish faux option to rev up your look.

Biker

Zippers and buckles

Quilted

Chic and comfortable

Jean Appeal

Your perfect wardrobe would include several pairs of jeans, right? They have wear-anywhere appeal and are one of the best "blank canvas" starting points for an outfit. From chillout daytime to superglam evening, jeans have it all.

Snug fit

Styling Tips

✽ Skinnies are denim BFs. Find a trusty pair to wear anywhere with anything.

✽ Try before you buy. Grab a handful of sizes and spend time in the changing room to find your perfect fit.

✽ Find a simple cut, then experiment with color and print for attention-grabbing style.

Skinny jeans are popular for a reason: they look ultrastylish on everyone! Try skinnies with stretch, or how about colorful denim? Wear your brights with white—it's guaranteed to get you noticed!

Boyfriend

Washed and worn look

Bootcut

Kick flare

Effortless chic is just a pair of denims away. This versatile style has become a wardrobe essential for a reason. Wear your boyfriend jeans with heels, ballet pumps, or high-tops for unexpected feminine chic!

Bootcuts have been around for decades, and why? They create a super flattering shape that balances out hips with a flare at the ankle. These shapely jeans look amazing with wedges or cowboy boots.

The LBD
aka The Little Black Dress

Let's talk about our favorite fashionable friend—the little black dress. Versatile, elegant, and perfectly stylish whatever the occasion … Every girl should own one! But what makes this wardrobe classic stand the test of time?

Classic

Sophisticated look

Styling Tips

✻ A classic LBD won't go out of fashion. Pick one that'll take you from decade to decade!

✻ Wear your babydoll with flip-flops for a smart daytime look, or rock it with extra bling for the perfect party outfit.

✻ Add pops of color with chunky jewelry or a bright blazer.

Back to Black

It's hard to imagine life without the LBD, but until the 1920s black was only ever worn in mourning. Thankfully, Coco Chanel's perfectly simple designs made their mark on the fashion world forever.

Fashion BF

Today, any shape or style will solve that last-minute style dilemma! This is one fashion BF that will always save the day (or night)! The LBD is a totally timeless fashion staple—whatever the trend!

Bodycon

Babydoll

Hourglass silhouette

Nipped-in waist

Classic Coats

It's all too easy to forget fashion when it comes to keeping warm. Wrapping up for winter can come in all shapes and sizes, from the classic trench coat, to the cute, woolen peacoat. Keep it chic with a statement style and you can't go wrong!

Styling Tips

* Go transseasonal and pick a trench for those in-between seasons when you can't quite predict the weather!

* Invest in a good quality piece that will last a lifetime. A navy peacoat is timeless.

* Go concert cool with a parka. Rock it day and night with shorts and rainboots.

Trench

 *Lightweight material*

Designed by Thomas Burberry in 1914, the trench coat was made for the military. The style was so wearable and flattering—it's no wonder it became such a fashion hit!

Pea

Double-breasted

Parka

Cozy and practical

With a woolen peacoat, you'll keep warm and stay smart, too! Originally worn by sailors, this double-breasted design with broad lapels (the collar parts) will give any outfit a classy edge.

This is the coat with wear-anywhere appeal that'll keep you totally toasty! Well, it had better—the Inuits invented this supercozy coat to keep them warm in the freezing Arctic!

Essential Footwear

Life is like a catwalk, and shoes are the ultimate 'runway' accessory. There is nothing like stepping out in a new pair of shoes for that instant 'happy feet' feeling. These three classic styles are certain to get fashionable toes tingling!

Stiletto

The ultimate heel

Styling Tips

* Stilettos suit anyone so don't freak out if you're no girly girl—they can look supercute with jeans and a T-shirt.

* Add wedges to your vacation packing list. They are summer's favorite shoe!

* Smart embellished ballet flats are a perfect alternative to heels for a special occasion.

It's the shoe that'll NEVER go out of style! Named after a dagger for its long, thin statement heel, the stiletto has been on fashion's most-wanted list for decades. In leather, suede, patent, or print, a stiletto heel will rock any outfit. You'll totally work the power strut in these!

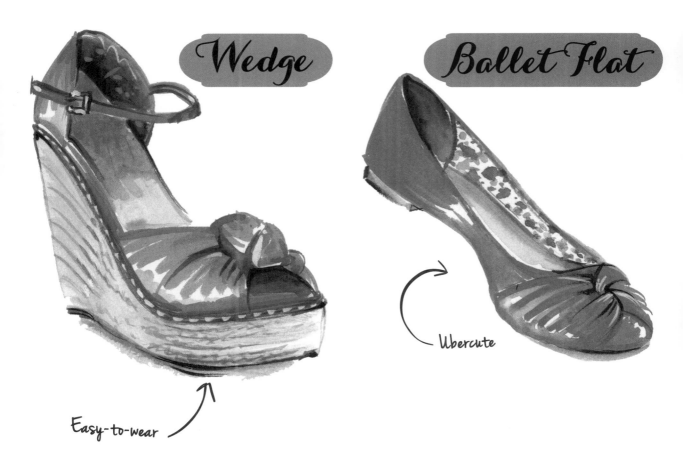

Wedge

Ballet Flat

Ubercute

Easy-to-wear

Not feeling it for flats, but don't want a pair of impossible heels to walk in? Then get your wedge on! Available in endless colors and shapes, wedges are perfect for adding no-hassle height! They will totally solve your what-to-wear footwear conundrums.

The simple and sweet choice—after all, they're inspired by ballerina shoes. Every girl has at least one pair, right? The ballet flat is the ultimate basic for feet, and if you want to push the fashion boundaries, add bling with bow, glitter, or jewel embellishments.

Arm Candy

Carrying it all has never looked so cool! Purses and bags are the ultimate arm candy, and some enduring classics continue to stand the test of time. Plus, there is a shape to suit every occasion, so there's no guilt in having at least three (or five!) is there?

Satchel

College cool

Styling Tips

✳ A real leather satchel can be expensive, but it's worth the investment—it'll last you a lifetime!

✳ Keep a tote folded up in your main purse for emergency use!

✳ A classic black clutch will go with almost anything and will look superslick.

So you want it all—vintage-cool AND practicality? A satchel is your purse solution! With its long adjustable straps and buckles, it has loads of room. Whether you're carrying books or your stash of daily essential items, the satchel will hold it all and keep your hands free!

Tote

Cheap and chic

Clutch

Party BF

Tote means "to carry," which makes sense! Usually made in canvas, a tote is THE must-have bag for when your purse is overflowing or you need an easy sling-on-your-shoulder option. And the best thing? There are loads of designs to choose from, so your bag can also carry a little bit of you!

Say hello to the party purse! When all you need to carry is keys, money, cell phone, and lipgloss, the clutch is where it's at. Lightweight, smart, and packed with style, tuck this neat little purse under your arm, and hit the dance floor! With plenty of bargains, it won't hurt your wallet to top off your look.

Fashion Quotes

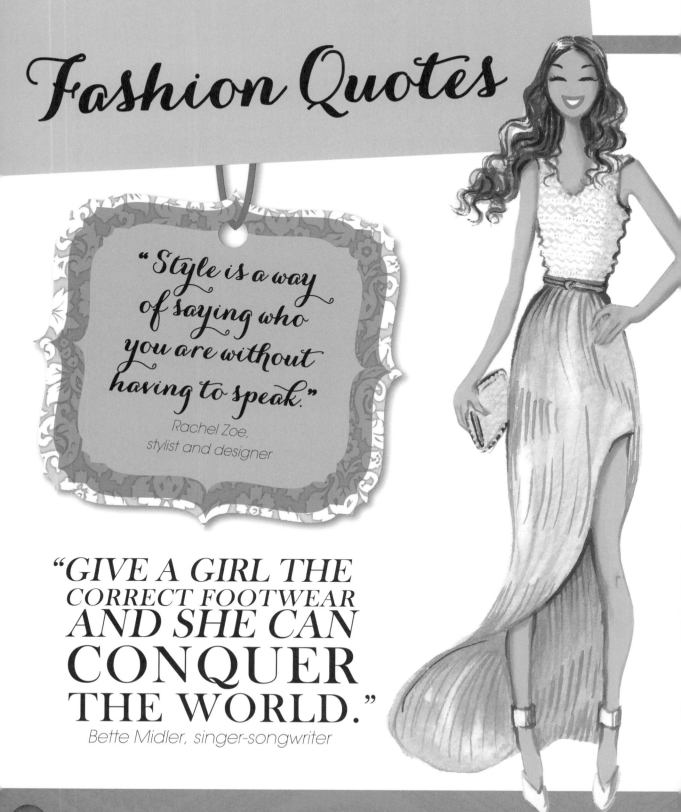

"Style is a way of saying who you are without having to speak."

Rachel Zoe,
stylist and designer

"GIVE A GIRL THE CORRECT FOOTWEAR AND SHE CAN CONQUER THE WORLD."

Bette Midler, singer-songwriter

" *Over the years I have learned that what is important in a dress is the woman who is wearing it.* "

Yves Saint Laurent, designer

"Fashion is not something that exists in dresses only. Fashion is in the sky, in the street, fashion has to do with ideas, the way we live, what is happening."

Coco Chanel, designer

"WHY CHANGE? EVERYONE HAS HIS OWN STYLE. WHEN YOU HAVE FOUND IT, **YOU SHOULD STICK TO IT.**"

Audrey Hepburn, actress

"I don't design **clothes.** I design **dreams.**"

Ralph Lauren, designer

Shopping in ... *London*

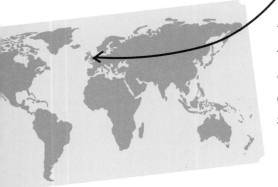

Think you know London? Breezing through the Underground and squeezing through the crowds won't make you a pro ... so get savvy and streetwise with the top three must-visit shopping locations.

Designer

Bond Street

Bond Street is the place to go for designer clothes, hands down! World famous for big-name designers, Bond Street is every fashionista's dream. Don't have the cash to splurge? There is nowhere better to window-shop!

Everyday

Oxford Street

Head over to Oxford Street for fast fashion that won't break the bank. With big brands and flagship stores, you're spoiled for choice! And don't forget the world-famous department store, Selfridges.

Vintage

Brick Lane

Find your dream retro outfit at the Brick Lane market or one of the amazing vintage shops in the area. East London is the perfect place to uncover fashion treasure!

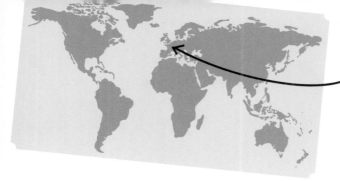

Paris

Do you have Parisian chic? Picking up a croissant for breakfast every morning and shouting *Bonjour* to friends won't mean you're in the know about where to go. Hotfoot it with the fashion elite and learn how to navigate the city, shopper-style!

Designer

Avenue Montaigne
Everyone knows that Paris is the home of fashion. On Avenue Montaigne, famous designers' stores line the street in charming old buildings. Take a stroll down beautiful Avenue Montaigne and you'll be in the center of style!

Everyday

Rue de Rivoli
There's a little something for everyone on Rue de Rivoli, from brands you'll know to awesome French department stores and souvenir stalls. Make it your go-to location.

Vintage

St-Ouen Flea Market
Paris is famous for its markets, and the St-Ouen market is huge. With 2,500 sellers, you're bound to spy a one-off piece—it's a thrifty person's heaven!

Ooh la la!

Shopping in ... New York

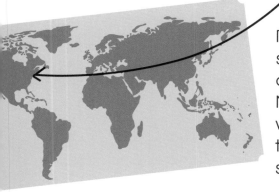

Ready to make a fashion cameo in the U.S. style capital? Slip into your highest heels, grab a bagel, and hail a yellow cab in NYC! If you want to rub shoulders with the Big Apple's 'It' crowd, these are the places to spend in.

Designer

5th Avenue

For straight-up glamor, there's only one destination—5th Avenue. With back-to-back designer names from Tommy Hilfiger to Jimmy Choo, Fendi to Armani, it's brand heaven!

Everyday

125th Street

Strut up to 125th Street. It's Harlem's central boulevard and THE go-to spot for clothing stores. Focus your shopping between St. Nicholas Avenue and 5th Avenue for all your favorites.

Vintage

Beacon's Closet

This vintage store in Williamsburg is so mind-blowing, it should come with a warning label. Packed with wall-to-wall vintage treasures, it's a once-in-a-lifetime shopping experience!

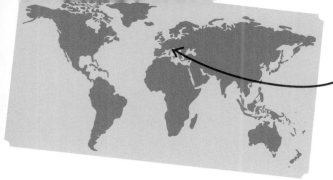

Milan

Wanna go all-out glamor in a city that's winning in the style stakes? If anyone knows how to pull it off to perfection, it's the Italians. If you want to try your hand at Itali-glam, Milan-style, you've got to know where to shop …

Designer

Quadrilatero d'Oro

Milan's best boutiques are centered around one legendary square of streets known as the Quadrilatero d'Oro, which means "rectangle of gold." Totally fitting, right? There are certainly plenty of precious finds for the sophisticated shopper.

Everyday

Armani Megastore

A designer label without the card-maxing costs. Too good to be true? Hunt down Armani Megastore and you'll see for yourself—catwalk fashion at seriously cheap prices. Oh, and it's massive, so don't stress—you WILL find a bargain!

Vintage

Vintage Delirium

For the retro wow factor, try Delirium. This incredible vintage showroom has fairy-tale clothes from every decade. Sidle up with celeb shoppers and top designers rummaging for inspiration. Hey, if it's good enough for Madonna, it's good enough for us!

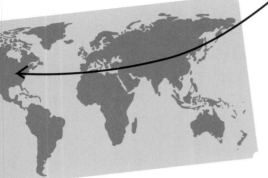

Shopping in ... Chicago

Want to get swept away by fabulous fashion in the Windy City? Then get your walking shoes on for a tornado trip down the bustling streets of Chicago for the best that Illinois has to offer.

Designer

"Magnificent Mile"

The designers begin between Michigan Avenue and Oak Street, where you'll find Prada and Bulgari among many famous names. But it doesn't stop there—the high-rise malls are home to plenty more must-visit boutiques.

Everyday

North Michigan Avenue

As you walk down the avenue toward the river, you'll find plenty of chain-store favorites to better suit your purse. And don't forget to visit Macy's at the Loop!

Vintage

VMR

Vintage, Modern, Resale is a vintage showroom with plenty of "wow"! This special store is appointment only, so you'll need to be prepared. If you're not ready for VMR, then head to the huge Lenny & Me store in Wicker Park.

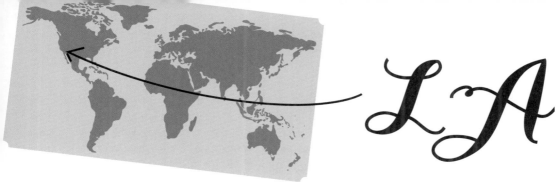

L·A

Get your shades on for some superstar shopping, LA-style. If you're thinking *Pretty Woman*, then you've still gotta lot to learn. Hollywood has every kind of fashion to tempt the stylish shopper!

Designer

Rodeo Drive
This iconic street in Beverly Hills is the center of luxury fashion in LA. With four blocks of sought-after stores, any fashionista will be spoiled for choice!

Everyday

Hollywood and Highland
Make a beeline for this epic shopping mall and you'll be in fashion paradise. The 387,000-square-foot center also houses theaters, nightclubs, and restaurants so visitors won't get bored!

Vintage

Jet Rag
If you are on the hunt for that special something at a bargain price and don't mind whiling away a few hours, then head directly to Jet Rag. This is definitely the place to indulge if you have a passion for thrifting!

Shop in Style

Rummaging, quick changes, and pounding the sidewalks—it's all in a day's work for a seasoned shopper. Find it hard to keep your glam on when you're bargain-hunting? Be a smart shopper and stylish to boot, with this what-to-wear guide.

1 A loose dress is ideal shopping wear. Stay away from lots of buttons or zippers to avoid major changing-room fatigue.

2 Lose the bulky purse and pick a satchel. This compact carryall won't interfere with your rummaging.

3 Make sure you wear the right bra to match what you are shopping for (or take it with you).

4 Top shopping? Pop on a pair of leggings under your dress to make light work of your quick changes.

5 Shopping for shoes? Remember to wear the right socks or pantyhose to avoid unhappy feet later. Thick socks are a must when you're trying on winter boots.

"Buy less, choose well."

Vivienne Westwood

6 If you're planning a long day out, ditch the heels—cute flats are where it's at.

1

2

5

3

4

6

Shopping Strategy

Try these insider tips to whip your closet into shape and get the most out of shopping for fashion.

SIGN UP

GET INTERNET SALE SAVVY, AND SIGN UP TO RECEIVE EMAIL ALERTS FROM YOUR FAVORITE STORES. YOU'LL GET THE **LATEST INFO** AND BE THE FIRST TO KNOW WHEN IT'S **SALE TIME!**

Don't bag a bargain, just because.

Sure it's supercheap but does it fit properly? Does it suit your style? Will it go with the clothes you already have? If the answer to any of these is no, then move on!

Know your measurements

You know your size, right? But what about your size 50 years ago? Vintage sizes can be baffling so make sure you know your bust, hip, waist, and inside leg measurements before you go rummaging.

Invest in quality

You don't need to spend big bucks all the time. Invest in several good-quality basic items, and your wardrobe will get an instant upgrade. Then mix up your everyday buys with one quality piece you LOVE.

Look online first

Before buying an expensive designer piece, check out online stores for a deal.

Check out department stores

They might be running a sale or you may find a discount coupon you can use on your big splurge!

Key Fabrics

Add texture to your trend and put some fabric know-how into practice.

Soft JERSEY
The knit fabric makes jersey so comfortable. It's a perfect match for the draped dress, since it won't crease and will keep you snug on a cold winter day.

Hardwearing DENIM
Denim is woven so that only half the threads are dyed, which is why real denim is dark on one side and white on the other. Uberversatile and hard-wearing, denim is an everyday fashion dream!

Cool COTTON
Woven and spun into a soft, breathable fabric, cotton is used for just about everything. A simple T-shirt, summer dress, or floral scarf, your wardrobe should be full of it!

See **pages 26–27** for how to work the leather jacket.

Cozy CASHMERE

Cashmere wool is strong, light, and oh-so soft, which is why it's become a fashion luxury. Invest in cashmere and you won't be disappointed!

Luxe LEATHER

Leather is as practical as it is stylish. It is a staple material for classy clothing and accessories. A quality leather jacket will last a lifetime.

Chic CHIFFON

Chiffon is a sheer, woven fabric. Number one for evening wear, chiffon always looks chic as it is so light and floaty. Try a chiffon maxi skirt to work the fabric by day!

Key Prints

Get your print on with eight of the most iconic patterns in fashion!

Novelty
Popular in the 1950s and still everywhere today. Patterns are often made bold and vibrant for standout style.

Geometric
A big hit in the 1960s, geometric prints look best on simple pieces like sweaters and leggings.

Check
Check can be called plaid or tartan and comes in pretty much every color.

Polka dots
Sharing its name with the dance form "polka," this playful print works on pretty much any style, shape, or fabric.

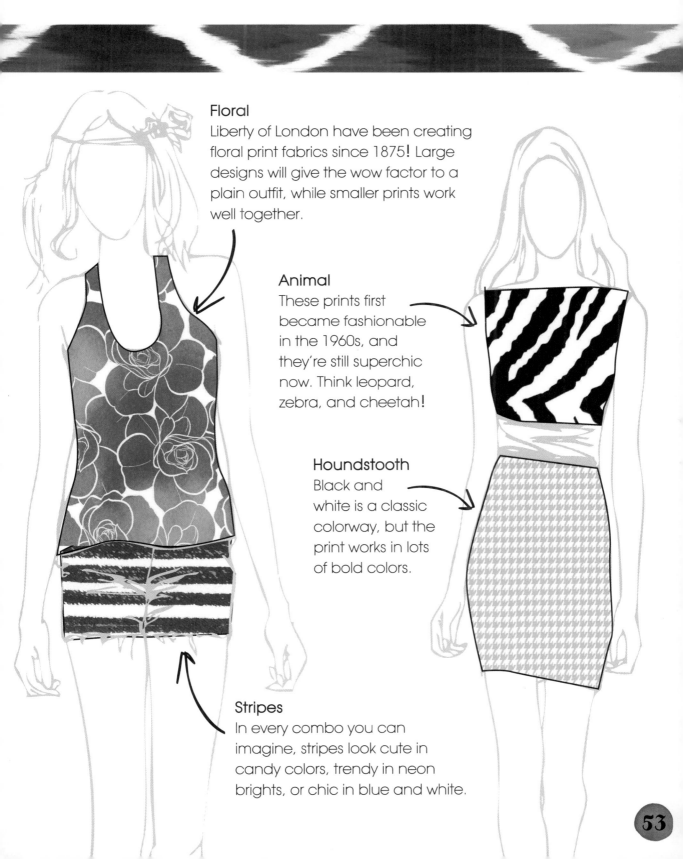

Floral
Liberty of London have been creating floral print fabrics since 1875! Large designs will give the wow factor to a plain outfit, while smaller prints work well together.

Animal
These prints first became fashionable in the 1960s, and they're still superchic now. Think leopard, zebra, and cheetah!

Houndstooth
Black and white is a classic colorway, but the print works in lots of bold colors.

Stripes
In every combo you can imagine, stripes look cute in candy colors, trendy in neon brights, or chic in blue and white.

Color Quiz

The right colors can turn a look from geek chic to front-row fashion in an instant, but which ones work for you? Try this 30-second quiz to see if you should be working the warms or getting runway-ready with cools!

1. In hot sunshine, you …

A) Tan easily
B) Burn quickly

2. What color are your eyes?

A) Blue, gray, deep brown, or black
B) Hazel, green, or light brown (or darker with light flecks)

3. Take a peek at the vein on the inner part of your arm. Is it:

A) A blue-green color?
B) A blue-purple color?

4. When it comes to jewelry, what's your must-have metal?

A) Gold
B) Silver

5. What's your natural hair color?

A) Red, reddish brown, strawberry blonde, or golden blonde
B) Black, light blonde, or brown with no red tones

6. What color T-shirt would you rock best?

A) Beige
B) White

Mostly As—WARM

You're all about warm colors: gold, yellows, oranges, browns, and warm reds. When you're planning outfits, the secret is to make these colors your key accents. You can still wear any color you like, but you'll look supergorgeous in warm shades. For instance, if you're rocking pink, go for a peachy pink rather than a purplish pink!

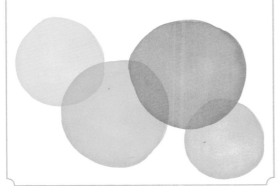

Mostly Bs—COOL

Cool colors are perfect for you: silver, blues, greens, purples, and blue-based reds. You can still look great in any color, but you'll REALLY shine in cool shades. Pick out block-colored dresses and scarves in your ideal shades. For example, if you're rocking blue, go for a sky blue instead of a warmer-looking turquoise.

A mixture of As and Bs—NEUTRAL

Did you get some of both? Lucky you, because you're probably neutral. You can look good in pretty much any color, and gold or silver jewelry both totally work on you. Mix it up to find what suits you best—try standing in front of a mirror, then hold fabrics up next to your face, and see what makes you pop and what washes you out!

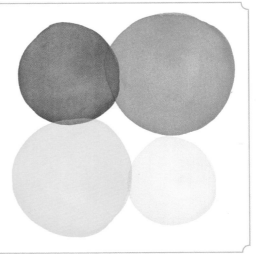

Shoestring Style

Love it when your clothes look awesome straight out of the closet, but hate it when they make you feel BLAH? These supersimple styling tips and tricks will totally update your look without breaking the bank!

Top socks
You simply can't ignore a cute pair of socks! Wear them bright and bold with pumps or sandals for standout style.

Pretty pinup
Bored with an old sweater? Find a cheap brooch in a thrift store and pin it to your knitwear. Brave that chilly fall weather in style!

Roll 'n' turn
Roll up the sleeves of an old T-shirt and try turning up your pants or shorts for a relaxed, off-duty vibe.

Button switch

Swap the buttons on an old cardigan with vintage finds to shout cozy, customized chic. Just make sure your new buttons fit the buttonholes!

Headgear

Make styling your strands less stressful with a handmade headband. Cut up an old T-shirt into strips and braid them together. Search online for hair how-tos.

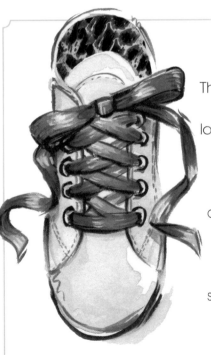

Rock it with ribbon

Thread ribbons through belt loops to create a makeshift belt, tie around a dress to pull in the waist, or pretty up sneakers by switching your laces with satin ribbon.

Shade chic

Switch on the glamor with supersleek shades. Whether you wear them or rock them hung over your collar, shades will add the cool factor to any outfit.

Customizing

Grown out of something you love or bored by a shabby, old outfit? Make it unique with these quick and easy ideas for customizing your clothes.

Cut yourself a cardigan

A sweater that's shrunk in the wash can be transformed into a cardigan with careful cutting. Use scissors to cut down the front in a straight line to create a quick-but-cute cover-up!

Just add lace

Give denim a new lease of life with pretty pieces of lace. Cut panels of lace material and sew into denim shorts. Try pieces in the pockets or triangle sections in the sides.

Bow beauty

Start a new season with a brand new hairdo. Ribbon is seriously cheap and a big bow will update your style from bedhead to preppy chic!

Fringe it!

For a fresh, summer festival look, find an old tank top or cut the sleeves off an old tee. Then simply snip strips from the bottom up to the middle of the top. Supereasy, right?

Get glittery

Scuffed shoes aren't slick but glitter footwear is fashion gold. Protect the floor with newspaper. Mix glitter with white glue and spread over the shoes. While the glue is still wet, sprinkle more dry glitter over for extra sparkle. Leave to dry overnight and add a clear layer of glue to seal in the glittery goodness!

Fashion Inspiration

Show off your fashion `personality`
Show the world who you are and how you feel. Your fashion choices reflect your pesonality, so rock your own unique look and buck the trends!

Embrace the unique
It takes a lot of bravery to bare your fashion soul so don't criticize someone else's choices. Embrace everyone else's unique style and they'll embrace yours!

Mix up your style!
Think worn-in basics and colorful, elaborate prints. Or go pretty-girl floral in a dress worn with boyish brogues for an edgy look!

Know that you're awesome, whatever you wear!
Dress in what makes you feel comfortable and your fashion confidence will rocket! In the end, it comes down to wearing what feels right.

Read blogs for inspiration

The Internet is full of supercool blogs written by girls just like you. Discover your favorite fashion feed for daily tips and advice. And hey, if you're really excited, why not start one of your own?

See pages 54–55 to find out which colors suit you.

Don't wear colors that don't suit you

Learn what colors suit you so that you can rock any off-duty look. Take the color quiz to learn which color group you're in, and play around with shades that look great on you.

Be nice to your body

Don't get hung up on the numbers! If one size doesn't fit you, grab another one—it's just not a big deal. Sizing varies from brand to brand anyhow, so be confident, NOT size-obsessed!

Don't be afraid to
break the rules!

The beauty of fashion is, there aren't any rules! Well, none that aren't made for breaking, anyway. Experiment with your style, and don't be afraid to take risks!

Style Tribe Quiz

Get your quiz on to find out
which style tribe you're in!

1. It's Sunday and you're chilling
   out with your friends.
   What are you wearing?

A) A floral dress and a cardigan.
B) Ripped, skinny jeans and your
   fave band T-shirt.
C) Boyfriend jeans and a
   comfy hoodie.
D) Bright leggings, a printed T-shirt,
   and statement jewelry.
E) Something quirky and new that
   you bought yesterday.
F) A vintage dress you found
   online.

C) Real-life stories. Ordinary
   people, crazy stories—what's
   not to like?
D) Street style. It's way more fun
   seeing real people work
   their own style.
E) Beauty. Finding dramatic new
   eye tricks is what it's all about.
F) Catwalk pics. You simply HAVE
   to know what will be hot
   next season.

2. You're looking through a
   fashion mag. What are your
   flick-to pages?

A) Everyday fashion. You're all
   about the cute dresses!
B) Music reviews. For the inside
   scoop on the latest releases.

Street Style
Check out this week's
top street style spots!

4. Your BF has got you surprise gig tickets. What's the music?

A) You don't mind but hopefully nothing too loud.

B) Rock or indie and you're happy.

C) Pop all the way.

D) Hip-hop or R 'n' B.

E) Something a little retro.

F) The new band you heard this week online.

5. If you had to pick a dream purse, what would it be?

A) A classic design that won't go out of style.

B) A leather backpack customized with badges and studs.

C) A funky canvas tote that you can sling on your shoulder.

D) A brightly colored oversized clutch.

E) Easy, a vintage Chanel bag.

F) Hmmm … can you have more than one? Like, for every day of the week?

3. What's your signature makeup look?

A) Pink blush and gloss to keep it cute.

B) Lots of eyeliner, then you're happy being seen in public.

C) Mascara, gloss, and go! You like the natural look.

D) Superbright, standout lippy to dial up the color.

E) Bring on the classic red lip. Gotta love the vintage look!

F) Whatever the hot new product of the moment is.

Turn the page to discover your style tribe.

Mostly As – TOTALLY GIRLY

Dress code = cute! A closet full of flirty dresses with ballet pumps to match. Pastels and florals are your staples and they totally work for you. Your style is very pretty so don't be afraid to grunge it up once in a while.

Mostly Bs – ULTIMATE ALTERNATIVE

Punk meets pretty with your edgy and alternative style. Think ripped denim, studs, and an endless supply of eyeliner! Your friends would describe you as a rock chick, but it's style with an edge for a supersweet girl.

Mostly Cs – TOMBOY CHICK

Carefree and cool, you're happiest in jeans and a hoodie. Easy off-duty dressing is your fashion mantra, but don't be afraid to experiment—an accessory like a print scarf can give you no-hassle fashion points!

Mostly Ds – UNIQUE URBAN

Reach for the shades, because your look is awesomely bold and bright. Inspired by street style, you can pull off chunky jewelry better than anyone—the bigger, the better! Follow your fave bloggers to keep your style fresh.

Mostly Es – VINTAGE VIXEN

Fire up the time machine, you have gorgeous retro style. If there was an award for hunting down one-of-a-kind looks, it would have your name on it. Why not look up vintage hairstyle how-tos to complete your look?

Mostly Fs – TRENDSETTER

You're definitely not Miss Play-it-safe! You know what's hot before your friends even know it exists, and your style changes so fast it could make you dizzy. Just remember—sometimes it's about what suits you rather than what's on trend.

Design it

Cute and Casual

Forget threadbare sweats and too-big tees—this is carefree and cool weekend wear with effortless style. Create three casual looks to die for ... Off-duty never looked so good!

Pick some patterns and fabrics

Design it

Red Carpet

Dream big! Is yours a frothy, empire line or an ultra-feminine silk silhouette? Pick your frock of choice and make sure it has A-list impact.

Pick silk, satin, or chiffon ...

Sparkle

Pretty princess?

69

Design it

Trendy Tourist

Check out international street-style blogs to get the fashion lowdown, then pick and mix to match the trends. You'll be breezing through historical sights and sashaying up skyscraper stairways at double speed.

Pick comfy basics

sightsee
in style

Design it

Fab Feet

Put a fashionable foot forward with some enviable shoe and boot designs. Kick your designer brain into gear with a chunky boot, ballerina flat, and a heel with attitude.

Boot up →

Pick laces, bows, or buckles

Slip-on style

Stack it high!

Design it

Shopping Trip

Stocking up on basics and rummaging for fashion finds is no walk in the park. Get set for a long day out and design some outfits for shop-hopping success.

Pick cool fabrics and layer it up

Seasoned shopper

Design it

On the Beach

Get your summer brain in gear to make this beachwear range anything but boring. Think 1950s-inspired shapes or cutting-edge, modern patterns.

Pick prints and cutout shapes

Am I beach-ready yet?

Get
ready,
set, swim

Design it

Bespoke Bags

Tote it all

Make it personal with a bag that's totally catered to YOU! Bling it up for a must-have accessory that oozes "style statement."

Pick leather, fabric, or synthetic

Cute clutch

Classy & classic

Design it

Concert Chic

Make a serious festival style statement with an eye-catching outfit. It's all about accessorizing the look, so don't leave home without some floral headgear and fabulous shades.

Pick florals and denims

I'm with
the band

Hippy chic

a

Mini Moodboard

Make like a designer and create a lookbook. Cut out magazine images, save celeb styles that give you fashion envy, and print the best parts from your fave blogs.

Stick on some style!

Mini Moodboard

Stylish Selfies

Think you've found your top fashion looks? Snap a selfie, print it out, and stick it in. In fact, take LOADS of pictures! Every occasion is your own private catwalk moment, so express the YOU in every outfit, then record it here.

Notes

Think of this as your little black book of fashion go-tos. Note down fashion inspiration on-the-go and refer back to it later.

Know Your Fashion

Note to self: Learn the fashion lingo and you'll be one up in the style stakes!

A-line
A skirt or dress that flows in the shape of a capital A—narrow at the top and wide at the bottom.

Androgynous
A look that is both masculine and feminine.

Avant-garde
A term used to describe something that's totally modern, crazy, and new.

Babydoll dress
A short, loose-fitting daywear dress, popular in the 1990s.

Ballet flat
A flat and delicate shoe, often made with ribbon edging.

Beanie hat
A head-hugging knit hat that channels grunge cool.

Bobby sox
Short ankle-grazing white socks that were essentials in the 1950s.

Bodycon
Short for "body conscious," clothes that are tight-fitting and show off the figure.

Bootcut jeans
Thigh-skimming jeans that flare out at the bottom, perfect for teaming with boots.

Bowler hat
A hard felt hat with a rounded top, popular in Britain for over a century.

Boyfriend jeans
Loose, oversized jeans, often decked out with pockets and zippers for boyish cool.

Capri pants
Slim-fit pants that range from knee to calf-length.

Chic
A French term that means "elegantly stylish."

Chiffon
Sheer woven fabric used for graceful, flowing evening wear.

Cloche hat
A small hat with a down-turned brim, popular in the 1920s and very French!

Clutch
A strapless, lightweight purse for partying. Looks great underarm or on the dance floor.

Corset
Strapless bodice with laces or hook and eye closures. Gives an hourglass shape.

Cosmopolitan
Multicultural and worldly quality.

Cotton
Soft, breathable fabric that's used for pretty much everything in fashion.

Couture
Custom-made clothes made to exact measurements with hefty price tags!

Couturier
A designer who makes original garments to order for private clients.

Crimping
Using a hot iron tool to style your hair into tight waves.

Culottes
Half-pants, half-skirt—for those times you can't decide! Cut to knee or calf-length.

Denim
Hard-wearing, woven fabric, traditionally in blue.

Designer
Upscale clothing or accessories made by a major fashion house.

Dior
French designer who transformed postwar fashion.

Distressed
A fabric effect with a worn-in, vintage look.

Double-breasted
Popular for coats and blazers.

Empire waist
A dress or shirt with a raised waist, usually just under the bustline.

Fashionista
An obsessed follower of fashion!

Faux pas
A false step. A fashion faux pas is a way of referring to a fashion fail.

Festifashion
Music festival styling. Denim cutoffs, fringed tops—you know the score.

Flannel shirt
A shirt made of soft, flannel fabric that often comes in a plaid pattern.

Fringing
A fabric effect that can look like shredding or tassels.

Go-go boots
Low-heeled, knee-high fashion boots that often came in patent leather.

Grunge
The wear-what-you-want, dressed-down style that originated in the Nineties.

Gucci
An Italian brand that's a long-time staple of pop culture and celebrity.

Headgear
Hats, fascinators, headbands—anything that adds glamor north of your neck.

High-tops
Sneakers with a higher top area that comes above the ankle.

Jersey
A comfortable, knit fabric, best for draped clothing.

Leather
Long-life material made from animal rawhide. Vegan or 'faux' leather is also available.

Leg warmers
Dancewear-inspired footless socks that were everywhere in the Eighties.

Monochrome
An all black-and-white outfit. So chic!

On-trend
Up to date with the latest fashion trends.

Parka
Down-filled, fur-lined, cozy jacket, perfect for laid-back cool.

Peacoat
Double-breasted jacket with broad lapels.

Peter Pan collar
A cute rounded collar design for blouses, dresses, or as a separate accessory.

Poodle skirt
A statement skirt in the shape of a huge circle, popular in the 1950s.

Prada
The 100-year-old understated Italian brand that leads the classic style stakes.

Prêt-à-porter
Ready-to-wear clothing bought off the rack.

Prints
Fabric patterns and designs. If color is the mood, prints are the personality.

PVC
A shiny, plastic fabric that's not for the shy! Popular for supertight dresses in the 1960s.

Ready to wear
All the clothes you buy now are ready to wear. It's a fashion term that means that they aren't tailored specially for you!

Saddle shoes
Low-heeled, casual shoe with a plain toe and distinctive—often color-contrasted—panel.

Satchel
A buckle-up bag with long, adjustable straps.

Scrunchie
Fabric-covered hair tie, usually boldly patterned and with major Eighties appeal.

Silhouette
The basic shape of an item or outfit.

Skinny jeans
Jeans that are tight from hip to toe.

Stiletto
A classic party shoe with a trademark long, superthin heel.

Toile
A test garment in a cheap fabric to do a trial run before using expensive fabric.

Tote
A canvas shoulder bag that usually comes with a statement pattern or design.

Transseasonal / transitional
Clothes that are perfect for when the seasons are changing.

Trench coat
Lightweight coat that traditionally comes in tan with a waist belt.

Trendsetter
A fashion leader who wears the latest looks before others have caught up with them.

Tres chic
Totally and utterly fashionable.

Tulle
A fine, lightweight netting often used for petticoats under dresses.

Vintage
Stylish, one-off pieces from decades past.

Waterfall blazer
A cute, fitted blazer with excess fabric that hangs down from the lapels.

Wedge
Shoes, sandals, or boots with no gap in the height-boosting sole between the heel and ball of your foot.

You're totally set ...

You've walked through the world of fashion, you're the style-savvy, trendsetting, experimental girl that you were born to be!

YOU KNOW YOUR SHAPE and the colors that look amazing on you,

BUT YOU'RE NOT AFRAID TO up the stakes and try that statement piece.

YOU'VE TOTALLY LEARNED THAT IT ISN'T COMPLETELY NECESSARY TO HAVE THAT NEW DRESS, NEW PAIR OF JEANS, OH, AND THOSE SHOES, RIGHT NOW. **KEY PIECES AND SAVVY STYLING IS THE WAY FORWARD!**

YOUR FASHION IS **UNIQUE** *AND YOU'RE NOT AFRAID TO WORK IT* **YOUR WAY.**

Drumroll please for the **brave.** the **bold,** and the **seriously stylish** ... YOU!